Nǐ Hǎo

④

Student Workbook

Advanced Level

by

Shumang Fredlein · Sitong Jan

ChinaSoft

Nǐ Hǎo 4 – Student Workbook – Advanced Level
First published 2001
Revised edition 2008; reprinted 2010
3rd edition 2012

ChinaSoft Pty Ltd   ABN: 61 083 458 459
P.O. Box 845, Toowong, Brisbane, Qld 4066, AUSTRALIA
Telephone (61-7) 3371-7436
Facsimile (61-7) 3371-6711
www.chinasoft.com.au

Written by Shumang Fredlein (林淑满), Sitong Jan (詹丝桐)
Illustrated & designed by Xiaolin Xue (薛晓林)
Software by Paul Fredlein
Edited by Linda Smith (陈亮吟), Christine Ko, Sitong Jan (詹丝桐)

Companion textbook, audio CDs and software are also available.

ISBN 978 1 876739 25 6

Foreword

This 你好 *4 Student Workbook* is a learning activity book based on the 你好 *4 Textbook – Chinese Language Course, Advanced Level*. It contains a variety of activities that provide opportunities for students to practise the four communication skills – listening, speaking, reading and writing.

Activities designed for a particular communication skill can be adapted for other skills to suit students' needs, e.g. the listening exercise can be used for speaking; the reading and writing exercises can also be used for listening and speaking. To resemble real life situations, the listening and reading materials sometimes contain unfamiliar words/expressions. Students can either deduce the meaning based on the context of the passage, or consult a dictionary.

The listening exercises are included in the *Teachers' Handbook* and recorded on audio CDs. The teacher may play the CD to the class, or alternatively, read out the passages from the *Teachers' Handbook*. Answers to all of the questions in this workbook are included in the *Teachers' Handbook*.

Chinese characters are used in conjunction with Pinyin to reinforce reading and writing skills. However, Pinyin is kept to a minimum. Students should write in characters wherever possible and only use Pinyin for unknown characters. The textbook lists the characters that students should learn to write. These characters are included in the 写字练习 section of this workbook. Students should always write characters in the correct stroke order and in good proportion. They should also develop an appreciation for beautifully written characters, i.e. the art of calligraphy.

Contents

第一课　又开学了

1-1-A Use complete sentences to answer the following questions.

1. 开学了，Mary 的心在哪里？

_____

2. 快开学了，你看 Linda 会开心吗？

_____

3. 开学了，John 的心收回来了吗？

_____

4. 开学了，Peter 的心收回来了吗？

_____

5. 你觉得时间过得快吗？

_____

6. 你认为做什么事的时候时间过得最快？

_____

7. 你认为做什么事的时候时间过得最^{màn}慢？

_____

8. 开学了，你的心收回来了吗？

_____

9. 开学了，你该怎么把心收回来？

1-1-B Rewrite the following sentences in Chinese, using 才……又…….

开学
了

1. It seems like the holidays have just started but it will soon be school again.

放假 才 开始，和 又 学校（开始）

2. You've just arrived and you're leaving already!

你 才 到了 和 又 出去.

3. My older sister bought a pair of shoes yesterday and she bought another pair today!

我姐姐 买 一双 新鞋

4. He just went to the movies this morning and is going again tonight!

他 上午 才 去 影 和 又 去。
电

1-1-C Rewrite the following sentences in Chinese, using 也.

1. Our form teacher is a conscientious teacher and he cares for his students.

我们的 班 主任　　也 关心 学生。

2. He is popular and also studies well.

他 有 明 也 学习 得 好!

3. The two of us are classmates and are also good friends.

我们 两儿 是 同学们 和 也 好 的 朋友。

4. We have too many exams and too many assignments.

我们 有 太多 考　　也 太多 功课。

5. She is a soccer fan and also a tennis fan.

她 是 一个　　　也

1-1-D Rewrite the following sentences using 把.

1. 请你拿(ná)这本书给他。

请你拿这本书把他给。

2. 请你关好门(mén)。

请你把门关好.

3. 他们收拾(shí)好东西了。

他们把东西收拾了.

4. 昨天我哥哥带女朋友回家见我爸爸和妈妈。

昨天我哥哥把朋友带回家把妈妈和爸爸见.

1-1-E Rewrite the following sentences in Chinese, using 把.

1. Go and finish your homework.

把作业去做好.

2. Please return the dictionary to me.

3. He put the computer in his own room.

4. My little brother ate all the ice cream.

5. I gave him my address.

1-1-F Write your questions then conduct a survey with your classmates about when they think time passes the fastest and the slowest.

Q1. _____

Q2. _____

Name		
(Yourself)		

List the two most common things mentioned for each situation.

1. 时间过得最快的时候是

_____

2. 时间过得最^{màn}慢的时候是

_____

1-1-G Rearrange the following into proper sentences.

1. 过得时间快真，下个了开学就要星期。

_____

2. 开学了，心可是的他回来没还收。

开学了，可是他心还没回来。

3. 好真开学，聊无了在家假放太。
_{liáo wú}

_____

4. 我们主任班今年的是师老科学。
_{zhǔ rèn}

我们班主任今年是科学老师。

5. 你人选觉得佳最班长的谁是？
_{xuǎn} _{jiā}

_____

6. 大家为认都老师教学英语认真很。

_____

7. 年今忙学习，活动的学校多也。

_____

8. 妈妈过来忙不担心，我们可是放心要她。
_{dān}

_____

9. 哥哥心开非常最近，因为朋友女交了个一他。

_____

10. 俩我们同学是同班，可是来谈不。
_{liǎ}

_____

6

1-1-H How do you say the following in Chinese? Write in characters wherever possible.

1. It seems the holiday just started and it is school again.

_____

2. He doesn't feel like coming back to school because his mind is still on holidays.

_____

3. Our form teacher this year is our math teacher.

_____

4. Our form/class teacher cares very much about the students.

_____

5. Our Chinese teacher is a conscientious teacher.

_____

6. Our English teacher told us to pull ourselves together and study hard.

_____

7. We will have a class meeting at three o'clock this afternoon.

_____

8. Everyone thinks he is the best candidate for class leader.

_____

9. There is too much work and he worries that he can't manage it all.

_____

10. We get along well and quickly become good friends.

_____

1-1-I Write the meaning of each word, then use the word to make a sentence.

		meaning	*sentence in Chinese*

1. 开始 ^{shǐ}　begin　　开始！

2. 开学　start school　　今天我学校开学.

3. 学习　study　　我学习中文.

4. 同学　classmate　　同学们都上学。

5. 认真

6. 认为　consider　　我现在认为吃饭。

7. 班主任 ^{zhǔ rèn}　form/homeroom teacher　　我班主任关心学生。

8. 班长　class leader　　我们班长很好.

9. 班会　class meeting　　今天有一个班会.

10. 开心　feel happy　　我今天开心。

11. 关心　care about　　我关心我朋友.

12. 热心　enthusiastic　　我今天很热心。

13. 担心 ^{dān}

14. 放心　stop worrying　　我说了"放心"。

1-1-J Answer the following questions in complete sentences.

1. 你们的班主任是谁？他／她人怎么样？
zhǔ rèn

_____

2. 你们的班长是谁？他／她人怎么样？

_____

3. 你觉得你们班上谁是班长的最佳人选？为什么？
jiā xuǎn

_____

4. 你想当班长吗？为什么？

_____

5. 你觉得你自己的人缘儿怎么样？
yuán

_____

6. 你们班上谁的人缘儿最好？为什么？
yuán

_____

7. 你今年学习忙吗？都忙些什么？

_____

8. 你妈妈在家里忙得过来吗？谁会帮她的忙？

_____

9. 你帮忙做家事吗？

_____

10. 在你们班，谁和你最谈得来？你们都谈什么？

1-1-K 你忙得过来吗？ Can you manage your day? Everyone has different living styles.
List your daily activities and explain how you manage your day.

时间	做什么事？

xuǎn 选一个	为什么？
忙得过来 huò 或 忙不过来	

1-1-L These are the personal files of three students in your class. Read the files and answer the questions.

Chén
陈利明

喜欢看电影，朋友多

学习还可以

lán
篮球打得很好

Lín
林真

热心，人缘儿好
　　　yuán

话不多，很喜欢音乐

学习认真，功课很好

运动马马虎虎
　　　　hǔ

Lǐ
李大成

外向，热心，有人缘儿
　　　　　　　yuán

学习不太好

喜欢运动，歌唱得好
　　　　　gē chàng

你觉得谁是班长的最佳人选？为什么？
　　　　　　　jiā xuǎn

谁不是班长的人选？为什么？

An election for school leader is coming up. Design a poster for your friend's election campaign.

1-1-M Read the following passage and answer the questions below.

又开学了。今年我们的班主任是学校新来的老师，也是我们的数学老师。班主任人非常好，非常客气，同学们都不怕他。

昨天下午第三节我们开班会，同学们选了王朋当班长。我觉得这是开玩笑，因为王朋学习不好，也常常没做作业。他的朋友不少，可是我觉得他的朋友都和他一样，爱玩儿，上课不认真。他篮球和网球都打得不错，可是他好像很忙，常常没来上课。我不认为王朋是班长的人选。

1. Who is the form teacher and how do students feel about him?

2. What does "怕" and "爱玩儿" mean?

3. How does the author value the new class leader?

4. Do you agree with the author's view and why?

1-1-N Write the characters that contain the given radical for each meaning.

1. 一　just _____; east _____; business, matter _____

2. 女　family name _____; to start _____; good _____; she, her _____

3. 讠　to recognize _____; to talk _____; to speak _____; to thank _____;

to test _____; to let (sb.) _____; please _____; lesson _____

4. 辶　to choose _____; to lose one's way _____; far _____; near _____;

to enter _____; to escort, to give _____; to pass, cross _____

5. 攵　to put, to let go _____; numbers, to count _____; to teach _____

1-1-O Use the given character to write the words for each meaning.

1. 放　to have a holiday _____; to finish class _____; to stop worrying _____

2. 开　to begin _____; feeling happy _____; to joke _____

3. 为　to become _____; think, consider _____;

mistakenly thought _____; because _____

4. 心　feeling happy _____; enthusiastic _____; to worry _____;

to care for _____; to stop worrying _____

5. 动　activity _____; sports, exercise _____; animal _____

6. 认　to think, consider _____; conscientious, earnest _____

1-1-P Listen to Peter's story and a short conversation, then answer the following questions.

1. Who is the person being described here?

2. What confusion do people have regarding his name?

3. How did Peter clarify the person's surname? Describe the process.

4. Write down his surname in character and describe its form in two ways.

Paste here the copy of the message given by your teacher and check your understanding.

1-2-A Answer the following questions using the information given.

1. Peter 参加什么课外活动？是什么时间？

4:00-5:30 pm

_____

2. Mary 参加什么课外活动？是什么时间？

6:00-7:00 am

_____

3. John 参加什么课外活动？他喜欢吗？

_____

4. Peter 参加什么课外活动？他喜欢吗？

_____

5. 他最讨厌的课外活动是什么？为什么？

_____

6. 学校今年增加了什么课外活动项目？

^{zēng} ^{xiàng mù}

_____

7. Kylie 想选哪个项目？

^{xuǎn} ^{xiàng mù}

_____

8. Ben 参加什么活动？要常练习吗？

^{liàn}

_____

9. Andy 参加什么活动？练习时间是什么时候？

^{liàn}

3:30-5:00 pm

_____

10. 他们多常练球？

^{liàn}

_____

1-2-B Rearrange the following into proper sentences.

1. 学校的活动他们课外下午星期三时间是。

_____

2. 活动的很多学校目^{mù}课外项^{xiàng}，同学每个都可以喜欢的选^{xuǎn}自己到。

_____

3. 参加你什么在课外学校活动？

参加你学校课外在什么活动？

4. 她入^{rù}足^{zú}球队^{duì}加，三次星期要练^{liàn}每个球每。

她入加足球，星期三要练球个次.

5. 加他学校的入^{rù}乐团^{tuán}交响^{xiǎng}，每个有两天练^{liàn}星期小提^{tí}琴^{qín}要。

_____

6. 打篮^{lán}球队^{duì}学校的很好我们得，比赛要常常加参。

_____

7. 学校有你们活动什么今年？

你们今年有什么学校活动？

8. 游园^{yóu yuán}下个月会的，我们打算班两个位^{wèi}摊^{tān}摆^{bǎi}。

9. 很多学校今年的活动，同学们忙都不得得了。

今年很多的学校活动，同学们忙得不得？

10. 大家很忙虽都然，忙但是很开心得。

1-2-C Rewrite the following sentences in Chinese, using 除了……以外.

1. Besides the soccer team, he also joined the basketball team.

_____

2. Besides tennis, she also likes playing table tennis.

_____

3. Everyone in my family likes Chinese food except my younger sister.

_____

4. All my friends joined the karate club except him.

_____

1-2-D Rewrite the following sentences in Chinese, using 虽然……但是…….

1. Although there are many activities, he doesn't like any of them.

_____

2. Although he and I are classmates, we don't get along well.

_____

3. Although that shirt is too tight, she still wears it often.

_____

4. Although I am extremely busy, I still call my mother every day.

_____

5. Although it was very cold, he still went swimming.

_____

1-2-E How do you say the following in Chinese? Write in characters wherever possible.

1. What extracurricular activities do you participate in?

   _____

2. I don't like extracurricular activities, but I have to choose one to participate in.

   _____

3. He is not happy because he cannot choose the activity he likes.

   _____

4. I joined the karate club and it is quite interesting.

   _____

5. My younger brother joined the rowing team and has to practise every day.

   _____

6. Our school has a sports carnival every year.

   _____

7. Is your school having a fete this year?

   _____

8. All the students in my class are going to that concert.

   _____

9. Our school is having a dance in October. Would you like to come?

   _____

10. I will participate in the high school science competition.

   _____

1-2-F Match each sentence and write it below.

1. 他虽然学习不好，

2. 除了星期天以外，

3. 我明天要考试，

4. 姐姐除了汉语以外，

5. 今年的课外活动我选了游泳，

6. 我加入了足球队，

7. 弟弟要参加科学比赛，

8. 今年学校活动很多，

A. 一个星期得练三次球。

B. 晚上得好好学习。

C. 可是我想我选错了项目。

D. 但是人缘儿很好。

E. 同学们都忙得不得了。

F. 他天天都要练球。

G. 也会说日语。

H. 现在天天都在做练习。

1. _____

2. _____

3. _____

4. _____

5. _____

6. _____

7. _____

8. _____

1-2-G Answer the following questions in complete sentences.

1. 你们学校有什么课外活动？

_____

2. 你觉得学校应该增加什么活动？

_____

3. 在学校，你参加什么课外活动？喜欢吗？

_____

4. 下课后，你有什么自己的活动？

_____

5. 在你的朋友中，谁的活动最多？他参加哪些活动？

_____

6. 谁加入了交响乐团？他们常练习吗？

_____

7. 你们学校哪个球队打得最好？他们常练习吗？

_____

8. 你参加过什么比赛？喜欢吗？

_____

9. 学校的游园会，你最喜欢哪个摊位？为什么？

_____

10. 你参加学校开的舞会吗？为什么？

_____

1-2-H Choose an appropriate word for each sentence, then use that word to write a sentence of your own.

正在　　虽然　　意思　　着　　高兴 (xìng)　　得 (děi)　　练习 (liàn)

1. 我们下个月要参加象棋 (xiàng qí) 比赛，现在天天都得 ＿＿＿＿＿＿＿。

＿＿＿＿＿＿＿＿＿＿＿＿＿＿＿＿＿＿＿＿＿＿＿＿＿＿＿＿＿

2. 姐姐现在正忙 ＿＿＿＿＿＿＿ 交男朋友。

＿＿＿＿＿＿＿＿＿＿＿＿＿＿＿＿＿＿＿＿＿＿＿＿＿＿＿＿＿

3. 爸爸网球打得不好，和他打球一点 ＿＿＿＿＿＿＿ 都没有。

＿＿＿＿＿＿＿＿＿＿＿＿＿＿＿＿＿＿＿＿＿＿＿＿＿＿＿＿＿

4. 弟弟 ＿＿＿＿＿＿＿ 做功课，不可以出 (chū) 去玩。

＿＿＿＿＿＿＿＿＿＿＿＿＿＿＿＿＿＿＿＿＿＿＿＿＿＿＿＿＿

5. 我这次数学考得不错，妈妈很 ＿＿＿＿＿＿＿ 。

＿＿＿＿＿＿＿＿＿＿＿＿＿＿＿＿＿＿＿＿＿＿＿＿＿＿＿＿＿

1-2-I Rewrite the following sentences in Chinese using 得 (dé, de, děi).

1. He eats a lot every day.

＿＿＿＿＿＿＿＿＿＿＿＿＿＿＿＿＿＿＿＿＿＿＿＿＿＿＿＿＿

2. My little sister caught the flu.

＿＿＿＿＿＿＿＿＿＿＿＿＿＿＿＿＿＿＿＿＿＿＿＿＿＿＿＿＿

3. Exam time is near and you must study hard.

＿＿＿＿＿＿＿＿＿＿＿＿＿＿＿＿＿＿＿＿＿＿＿＿＿＿＿＿＿

1-2-J Listen to the conversation between 李大中 (Lǐ) and 王红 (Wáng), then answer the following questions.

1. What time did 李大中 arrive at school and why did he arrive at that time?

2. Does 大中 like the activity he participates in? How often does he practise?

3. Will 王红 join the same activity? Give reasons.

4. Why do you think 王红 was elected as class leader and what does 王红 think of this?

Paste here the copy of the conversation given by your teacher and check your understanding.

1-2-K Write the characters that contain the given radical for each meaning.

1. 阝　except _____; team _____; cloudy, negative _____; sun, positive _____

2. 灬　like that _____; hot _____; to photograph _____

3. 氵　alive, to live _____; swim _____or_____; sea _____; port _____;

bay _____; a negative word _____; steam, vapor _____; thirsty _____;

Chinese (name of a dynasty) _____

4. 纟　to practise _____; fate _____; to give _____; red _____; green _____;

grade, level _____; to pass through _____

5. 亻　but _____; to live _____; low _____; you _____; he, him _____;

alike, resemble _____; to rest _____; measure word for clothes _____

6. 厶　to participate _____; to be able to _____; broadcasting station _____

7. 力　to add, to increase _____; to move _____; to do, to manage _____

8. 八　pleasure _____; together _____; public _____; minute _____

9. 日　hour _____; yesterday_____; tomorrow _____; sunny _____; late _____;

early _____; spring _____

10. 扌　grammatical word _____; to hit, to play _____; to pull, to play_____; row, to

line up _____; to look for _____

1-2-L The following are the activities you did last week. Write a short passage about your activities using as many of the given words/expressions as you can.

Monday　　Tuesday　　Wednesday　　Thursday　　Friday　　Saturday　　Sunday

xiàng mù　　xuǎn　　　　　liàn　　　　fù　　　　　　　　　　　　　　　　　bǎi

项目，选，活动，练，复习，最近，参加，又，过，舱锻，摆，忙着，

shè jì

设计，不得了，有意思，热心，帮忙，开始，打篮，除了……以外，

1-3-A Answer the following questions according to the information given.

1. Donald 用电脑做什么？

_____

2. Sally 用电脑做什么？

_____

3. 你看 Peter 在做什么？

_____

4. 你看 Claire 在做什么？

_____

5. 你看 Ron 是在写作业吗？

_____

6. Anna 最喜欢上网做什么？

_____

7. Kelvin 的爸爸常常上网吗？

_____

8. Michael 多常上网？

_____

9. Emma 最喜欢怎么和朋友联系？

_____

10. 他爸爸不准他做什么？

_____

1-3-B How do you say the following in Chinese? Write in characters wherever possible.

1. I changed my email address. This is the new one.

_____

2. I bought two CD-ROM games yesterday.

_____

3. I am addicted to computer games lately.

_____

4. I often go on the internet to search for information.

_____

5. I did not get on the internet yesterday, because my computer broke down.

_____

6. I sent an email to a friend in China last night.

_____

7. My father scolded me for always logging in to the chat room.

_____

8. His girlfriend sends him text messages all day long.

_____

9. Computers have a lot of functions and we should make good use of them.

_____

10. This is my website; you can log on and have a look.

_____

1-3-C Answer the following questions in complete sentences.

1. 你都用电脑做什么？你有自己的电脑吗？

_____

2. 你家有没有传真(chuán)机？谁最常用？

_____

3. 你常玩电子游戏(yóu xì)吗？为什么？

_____

4. 你多常上网？都上网做什么？

_____

5. 你的电子邮址(zhǐ)是什么？你的邮件多吗？

_____

6. 你觉得上网聊天很浪费(làng fèi)时间吗？为什么？

_____

7. 你们班有网页(yè)吗？你觉得这个网页(yè)有用吗？

_____

8. 你觉得电脑最好的功能是什么？

_____

9. 你平常都怎么和朋友联系(lián xì)？

_____

10. 你的手机有什么功能？

_____

1-3-D Write your questions then conduct a survey with your classmates about what they mostly use the computer for and how often they surf the net.

Q1. _____

Q2. _____

Name	Computer usage	Net surfing
(Yourself)		

Answer the following questions according to the results of your survey.

1. 常用电脑做功课的有几个人？

_____

2. 天天上网的有几个人？

_____

3. 不常上网的有几个人？

_____

1-3-E Find and circle words and phrases.

认 为 教 不 得 了 非 常 谈 正
真 课 人 真 岸 参 加 虽 然 在
向 放 关 开 学 练 但 方 交 姓
帮 假 心 交 始 习 是 便 朋 邮
多 忙 意 算 正 问 上 网 友 游
半 思 电 脑 带 但 地 址 喝 相
着 是 影 话 运 机 疼 病 高 兴

words/phrases	meaning in English	words/phrases	meaning in English

1. _____ _____

2. _____ _____

3. _____ _____

4. _____ _____

5. _____ _____

6. _____ _____

7. _____ _____

8. _____ _____

9. _____ _____

10. _____ _____

11. _____ _____

12. _____ _____

13. _____ _____

14. _____ _____

15. _____ _____

16. _____ _____

17. _____ _____

18. _____ _____

19. _____ _____

20. _____ _____

21. _____ _____

22. _____ _____

23. _____ _____

24. _____ _____

25. _____ _____

26. _____ _____

1-3-F Use each word/phrase to write a sentence. Include as many characters as possible.

1. 电脑 _____

2. 传^{chuán}真 _____
传真

3. 资料 _____
   ^{zī liào}

4. 电子邮件 _____

5. 电子游戏 _____
   ^{xì}

6. 电子邮址 _____
   ^{zhǐ}

7. 光盘 _____
   ^{guāng pán}

8. 一天到晚 _____

9. 网友 _____

10. 上网 _____

11. 网址 _____
    ^{zhǐ}

12. 网页 _____
    ^{yè}

13. 浪费 _____
    ^{làng fèi}

14. 手机 _____

15. 利用 _____

1-3-G This is the message 王红 sent you. Read her message and answer the questions.

xx: 你好！

今天发电子邮件给你，发了两次都发不出去，所以就发这份传真给你了。

你今年参加了什么课外活动？忙吗？我今年加入了学校的交响乐团。平常除了乐团要练习以外，我自己每个星期还要上两次小提琴课。最近同学们又选我当班长，我现在忙得不得了。

明天开始，我还要帮我妈妈的合唱团设计一个网页。我除了要写东西介绍她们的合唱团以外，还要帮她们拍照。虽然忙，但是我觉得忙得挺有意思的。等网页设计好了，我会告诉你她们的网址，你可以上网看我的设计。

你最近常上网吗？都上网做什么？

王红

1. By what means did 王红 send you this message and why did she choose this method?

2. What has 王红 been doing?

3. What does she hope you will soon see and how will you see it?

4. What did she want to know about you?

1-3-H Now, you reply to 王红 via email.

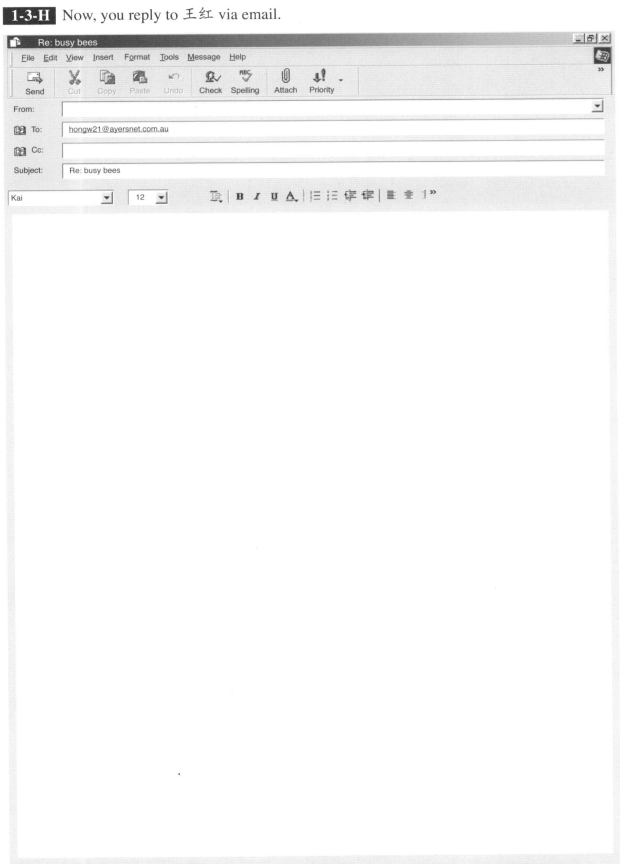

1-3-I Write the characters that contain the given radical for each meaning.

1. 十　really _____; to sell _____; south _____; thousand _____

2. 阝　mail _____; that _____; all, even _____

3. 月　brain _____; abdomen _____; fat, plump _____; clothes _____;

   friend _____; period _____; to have, there is/are _____

4. 冂　net _____; same, together _____; to use _____

5. 讠　should _____; speech _____; language _____; to speak, to tell _____;

   who, whom _____; test, to try _____; let, to allow _____; to recognize _____

6. 禾　sharp, to benefit _____; science _____; autumn _____; and, with _____

7. 土　location, site, address _____; floor, ground _____; place where people gather

   _____; town _____; dollar, piece _____; bad, to go bad _____;

   at, on, in _____; to go, last (year) _____

8. 一　no, not _____; flat, level, ordinary _____; again _____; two _____;

   five _____; to come _____; elder brother _____

9. 巾　to help, to assist _____; to take, to bring _____; teacher _____

10. 王　to play, to have fun _____; ball _____; texture, reason, logic _____;

    class, duty _____; present _____

第二课　有朋自远方来

2-1-A How do you say the following in Chinese? Write in characters wherever possible.

1. Our school has seven new teachers this semester.

    _____

2. The two of us talk about everything.

    _____

3. I don't have a good impression of that place.

    _____

4. People are friendly in Beijing.

    _____

5. Traffic conditions are very good here.

    _____

6. The air is fresh and the scenery is beautiful there.

    _____

7. I like travelling to places around the world.

    _____

8. He is not used to western foods.

    _____

9. I must go and experience different customs and practices.

    _____

2-1-B Answer the following questions in complete sentences.

1. 你们学校有交换老师吗？是从什么地方来的？

_____

2. 她对这个地方的印象怎么样？

_____

3. 你对西安的印象怎么样？

_____

4. 你觉得这儿的交通怎么样？

_____

5. 你觉得上海的交通怎么样？

_____

6. 你觉得北京的风景怎么样？

_____

7. 你住的地方风景怎么样？

_____

8. 你住的地方空气怎么样？

_____

9. 你去过的地方，哪儿给你的印象最深？为什么？

_____

10. 他是来学习还是来玩儿？

_____

2-1-C Write your questions then conduct a survey with your classmates about their impression of Beijing and what they think about the traffic and the air there.

Q1. _____

Q2. _____

Q3. _____

Name	Impression	Traffic	Air
(Yourself)			

Answer the following questions according to the results of your survey.

1. 对北京印象好的有几个人？

_____

2. 认为北京交通好的人多吗？有几个人？

_____

3. 认为北京空气差的人多吗？有几个人？

2-1-D Rearrange the following into proper sentences.

1. 我个学校们有三北京的来学生交换。^{huàn}

我们学校有三个北京的交换学生.

2. 好我他是和朋友，我不谈们俩无所。^{liǎ wú}

他和我是好朋友，我们俩无不所谈.

3. 妈姐妈对印象姐的男朋友不错。

妈妈印象对姐姐朋友不错.

4. 我两次他见过虽然，对他印象但是没什么。

虽然我见过他两次，但是印象对他没什么.

5. 气候里宜人这，很人也友善们。^{shàn}

这里气候宜人，也

6. 他北京的空气说差，不行人车也让。^{ràng}

7. 觉我交通上海得的很乱。^{hǎi　luàn}

8. 我利用想世界放假时旅行到各地。

9. 们中国他一人家不都习惯吃菜。

10. 我时旅行去美国们，多半饭馆到中国吃饭。^{měi}

2-1-E Choose an appropriate word for each sentence, then use that word to write a sentence of your own.

对　十分　多半　印象　告诉　^{ràng}让　各种　^{huàn}交换　^{dìng}一定

1. 姐姐有 ＿＿＿＿＿＿＿＿＿ 不同的^{xié}鞋。

＿＿＿＿＿＿＿＿＿＿＿＿＿＿＿＿＿＿＿＿＿＿＿＿＿＿＿

2. 我去年学习不好，今年 ＿＿＿＿＿＿＿＿＿ 要好好儿学习。

＿＿＿＿＿＿＿＿＿＿＿＿＿＿＿＿＿＿＿＿＿＿＿＿＿＿＿

3. 他的女朋友 ＿＿＿＿＿＿＿＿＿ 他很好。

＿＿＿＿＿＿＿＿＿＿＿＿＿＿＿＿＿＿＿＿＿＿＿＿＿＿＿

4. 他下个月要去上^{hǎi}海当 ＿＿＿＿＿＿＿＿＿ 学生。

＿＿＿＿＿＿＿＿＿＿＿＿＿＿＿＿＿＿＿＿＿＿＿＿＿＿＿

5. 我们今年的数学老师对我们 ＿＿＿＿＿＿＿＿＿ 客气。

＿＿＿＿＿＿＿＿＿＿＿＿＿＿＿＿＿＿＿＿＿＿＿＿＿＿＿

6. 爸爸对北京的 ＿＿＿＿＿＿＿＿＿ 不错。

＿＿＿＿＿＿＿＿＿＿＿＿＿＿＿＿＿＿＿＿＿＿＿＿＿＿＿

7. 这件事^{qíng}情你不要 ＿＿＿＿＿＿＿＿＿ 我妈妈。

＿＿＿＿＿＿＿＿＿＿＿＿＿＿＿＿＿＿＿＿＿＿＿＿＿＿＿

8. 这里的车会 ＿＿＿＿＿＿＿ 行人。

＿＿＿＿＿＿＿＿＿＿＿＿＿＿＿＿＿＿＿＿＿＿＿＿＿＿＿

9. 他星期天早上 ＿＿＿＿＿＿＿ 十点才起^{chuáng}床。

＿＿＿＿＿＿＿＿＿＿＿＿＿＿＿＿＿＿＿＿＿＿＿＿＿＿＿

2-1-F Do your own research and with the help of your teacher, list the scenic spots and historical sites of the following places.

北京 _____

_____

上海 _____
<small>hǎi</small>

_____

西安 _____

_____

<small>Hángzhōu</small>
杭州 _____

_____

<small>Niǔ yuē</small>
纽约 New York _____

_____

<small>Jiù jīn</small>
旧金山 San Francisco _____

_____

<small>Lún dūn</small>
伦敦 London _____

_____

<small>Tái</small>
台北 _____

_____

2-1-G Write the characters that contain the given radical for each meaning.

1. 口　　towards _____; may, approve _____; tell, inform; announce _____;

   right (location) _____; to eat _____; to drink _____; to sing _____;

   to be called, call _____; to vomit _____; to listen, to hear _____

2. 饣　　shop, building _____; cooked rice, meal _____; dumpling _____;

   to drink _____; biscuit, cake _____; hungry _____

3. 田　　boundary, extent _____; think, consider _____; man, male _____

4. 心　　to think _____; to feel, sense _____; you _____

5. 禾　　kind, type, sort _____; autumn, fall _____; sharp _____; science _____

6. 彳　　all right, to walk _____; toward, to _____; street _____; very _____

2-1-H Use the given character to write the words for each meaning.

1. 期　　term, semester _____; week _____

2. 地　　every region _____; place _____; geography _____

3. 气　　angry _____; air _____; weather _____

4. 行　　luggage _____; travel _____; pedestrian _____;

   not OK _____

5. 习　　get used to _____; to practise _____; to study, to learn _____

2-1-I 高利 is an exchange student from China. Listen to his conversation with 王红, then answer the following questions.

1. How has 高利 adapted to life here?

2. What is his impression of this place?

3. How does he keep in touch with people back home?

Paste here the text given by your teacher and check your understanding. You may also do a role-play with your partner.

2-2-A How do you say the following in Chinese? Write in characters wherever possible.

1. My parents hope that I take the opportunity to practise Chinese.

   _____

2. We invited a few friends to the park nearby for a barbecue yesterday.

   _____

3. They prepared plenty of food yesterday.

   _____

4. We will have sausages, steak and salad for dinner.

   _____

5. Today is so hot that it is a good day to go swimming.

   _____

6. We ate and chatted and all had a great time.

   _____

7. Some people in the park are playing tennis while some are playing soccer.

   _____

8. The guests are gone. Let's tidy things up!

   _____

9. Empty bottles, empty cans and newspapers are all recyclable.

   _____

10. Please help me put the rubbish in the bin!

   _____

2-2-B Use "有的……有的……" to rewrite the first two sentences in Chinese, then write two sentences of your own.

1. Some students in our class are doing the work while some are talking.

   _____

2. Some of these clothes just fit me while some are too small.

   _____

3.

   _____

4.

   _____

2-2-C Use "一边……一边……" to rewrite the first two sentences in Chinese, then write three sentences of your own.

1. He is used to listening to music while doing his homework.

   _____

2. My father likes to read the newspaper whilst having breakfast.

   _____

3.

   _____

4.

   _____

5.

   _____

2-2-D Write questions and conduct a survey to find out if your classmates like barbecues and their favorite place for a barbecue.

Q1. _____

Q2. _____

Name	Barbecue	
	✓or ✗	Where
(Yourself)		

Answer the questions according to the results of your survey.

1. 喜欢烤肉的有几个人？

_____

2. 大家最喜欢在哪里烤肉？

_____

2-2-E Rearrange the following into proper sentences.

1. 我的昨天生日是，请了我同学几个去一起看电影。

_____

2. 六个星期上，一家人我们去公园附^{fù}近的肉烤。

_____

3. 天气凉快很今天，是烤好肉的天气。

_____

4. 上个六我朋友到星期家里包^{bāo}们请饺子。

_____

5. 我们爸爸一边不让^{ràng}吃饭看电视一边。

_____

6. 把准备晚餐^{cān}妈妈好了，也都回来了大家。

_____

7. 下课后她都每天帮收拾老师东西。

_____

8. 地上不要垃^{lā}圾^{jī}丢^{diū}在，请垃^{lā}圾^{jī}桶^{tǒng}丢^{diū}到里。

_____

9. 可以利用报^{bào}纸^{zhǐ}回收再，放到里应该回收桶^{tǒng}。

_____

10. 今天热十分天气，放学后所以我们去就游泳。

_____

2-2-F Answer the following questions in complete sentences.

1. 她请朋友做什么？

_____

2. 烤肉时，他最不喜欢做什么？

_____

3. 他们今天喝什么饮料？
   yǐn liào

_____

4. 你常去公园吗？都去做什么？

_____

5. 你请朋友到家里吃饭吗？都吃什么？

_____

6. 你觉得烤肉方便吗？为什么？

_____

7. 你烤肉时通常吃什么？

_____

8. 你在家里帮忙收拾东西吗？为什么？

_____

9. 你家里哪些东西是可以回收的？

_____

10. 你帮忙做回收吗？为什么？

_____

2-2-G　Write questions and conduct a survey with your classmates to find out if they favor recycling and what they recycle at home.

Q1. _____

Q2. _____

| Name | Recycle | |
	✓ or ✗	What
(Yourself)		

Answer the questions according to the results of your survey.

1. 做回收的有几个人？

_____

2. 回收最多的东西是什么？

_____

2-2-H Your class is having a barbecue lunch in the park. List the food and drink needed and design some after-lunch activities.

吃 的：

喝 的：

活 动：

2-2-I Based on "带个盘子去" on page 42 in the Textbook, rewrite the story in your own words. Use as many characters as possible.

_____

_____

_____

_____

_____

_____

_____

2-2-J Read the story about 李大中 's party and answer the questions.

今天晚上李大中的父母因为有事出去，大中就请了十几个同学去他家听音乐。七点左右，同学们都到了。Ben 还带来了两包巧克力。

今天大中家没有咖啡，也没有汽水或可乐。大中就请大家喝乌龙茶。同学们喝了几口，有的人说还可以，有的人一点儿都不喜欢。Ben 看到冰箱里大中爸爸的啤酒，就拿啤酒给大家喝。

同学们一边吃喝一边听摇滚乐，大家都很开心。吃了巧克力，有的人去打电子游戏，有的人开始跳舞。十一点五十七分，大中说他父母亲快回来了。同学们就帮忙把空瓶子、空罐子和垃圾，都丢到垃圾桶里。十二点，同学们和大中说再见，就都回去了。

1. Why did 大中 hold a party and how long did it last?

2. How did they enjoy the food and drink? Give a detailed description.

3. What troubles do you think 大中 may face after his parents arrive home?

4. What advice would you give 大中 if he holds another party? Explain your reasons.

2-2-K Write the characters that contain the given radical for each meaning.

1. 巾　to hope _____; to help, to assist _____; to take, bring _____; teacher _____

2. 囗　garden _____; cause, reason _____; to return _____; nation _____

3. 冫　standard, accurate _____; time (frequency) _____; cold _____; cool _____

4. 夂　to prepare _____; every, each _____; slip _____; winter _____;

   summer _____

5. 攵　to collect _____; to teach _____; numbers, to count _____; to put _____

6. 王　to expect _____; ring, to surround _____; now, present _____;

   to play _____; ball _____; texture, reason, logic _____; class _____

7. 亠　related by blood _____; to forget _____; away, from _____; six _____;

   capital _____; merely, at once _____

2-2-L Use the given character to write the words for each meaning.

1. 机　chance, opportunity _____; aeroplane _____; airport _____

2. 园　park _____; zoo _____

3. 收　recycle _____; pack, put in order _____

4. 乐　cola _____; happy _____; music _____

5. 排　steak _____; volleyball _____; to queue up _____
   ^pái

6. 以　later, afterwards _____; therefore _____; thought (mistakenly) _____

2-3-A How do you say the following in Chinese? Write in characters wherever possible.

1. Everything is fine here.

_____

2. They are kind to me and treat me as a family member.

_____

3. There are two students in our class who like making trouble.

_____

4. Most students in his class study hard.

_____

5. I wrote a letter to a good friend last night.

_____

6. Our house is big and spacious.

_____

7. His swimming pool is heated by solar power.

_____

8. I had a photo taken together with my teacher at the school fete yesterday.

_____

9. The giant panda is a unique animal of China.

_____

10. She went to bed late last night and looks listless today.

_____

2-3-B Answer the following questions in complete sentences.

1. 他上课用心吗？

_____

2. 她上课在做什么？

_____

3. 你班上的同学上课用心吗？

_____

4. 你学习认真吗？

_____

5. 你冬天游泳吗？为什么？

_____

6. 他们怎么做环保？

_____

7. 你们怎么做环保？

_____

8. 在你家，谁最浪费水？为什么？
làng fèi

_____

9. 在你家，谁最浪费电？为什么？

_____

10. 放假时，你喜欢到各地走走吗？你最想去什么地方？

_____

2-3-C Rewrite the following sentences in Chinese, using 一切.

1. Everything is fine here. Please don't worry.

_____

2. For tomorrow's fete, we have everything prepared.

_____

3. You are home alone. Be careful with everything.

_____

2-3-D Rewrite the following sentences in Chinese, using 几乎 ^{hū}.

1. I am almost as tall as my father.

_____

2. My little brother is late for school almost every day.

_____

3. Mum was worried and hardly slept last night.

_____

4. I was so hungry that I could hardly walk.

_____

5. My older brother did hardly anything all day today.

_____

6. She hardly ate at the barbecue yesterday.

_____

2-3-E Rearrange the following into proper sentences.

1. 我们认真班学习同学的都多半很。

_____

2. 同学几个发^{wèn}问班我们有爱^{ài}上课很。

_____

3. 我一切好这儿都很，放请心。

_____

4. 他们对我好很都，把人我当自己。

_____

5. 加温^{wēn}他们的家利用游泳池^{chí}的是太阳^{yáng}能。

_____

6. 现在都不错大家做得环保。

_____

7. 动物都和特有的澳^{ào}大利亚^{yà}考拉^{lā}是袋鼠^{dài shǔ}。

_____

8. 弟弟什么几乎^{hū}吃没今天东西都。

_____

9. 爸爸、出去^{chū}事妈妈有了，只有个人一自己我在家。

_____

10. 我利用打算到走走各地春假。

_____

2-3-F Match the sentences and write them below.

1. 哥哥昨天写了三封信，	A. 一边看小说。
2. 我这儿一切都很好，	B. 回收做得很好。
3. 她上英语课时一边上课，	C. 给他的女朋友。
4. 他虽然上课不用心，	D. 几乎^{jī hū}什么东西都没吃。
5. 这儿的人很重视^{zhòng}环保，	E. 我打算去公园打球。
6. 妹妹今天不舒服，	F. 请放心。
7. 我们大家都是自己人，	G. 但是数学考试考得很好。
8. 功课做好以后，	H. 请不要客气。

1. _____

2. _____

3. _____

4. _____

5. _____

6. _____

7. _____

8. _____

2-3-G Listen to the conversation between 李大中 and 王红, then answer the following questions.

1. Where did 李大中 go and how did he feel about the place?

2. With whom did he go and what did they do there?

3. Who did he meet there? Describe their relationship.

4. How was 大中 received and what was his impression of the place?

Paste here the text given by your teacher and check your understanding. You may also do a role-play with your partner.

2-3-H Read the passage about 王红's day and answer the questions.

　　黄美英是班上新来的同学。今天是她的生日，她请了我和班上的几个同学去她家烤肉。

　　美英家很大，有很漂亮的客厅，五个房间，一个书房，三个浴室和四个厕所。院子里还有一个游泳池和一个网球场。

　　美英的父母非常客气，准备了很多吃的东西，有烤香肠、肉串、沙拉、面包和水果，大家都吃得很开心。我告诉美英我很美慕她有这么好的房子，可是美英说她家只有爸爸、妈妈和她三个人，住这么大的房子太冷清了。她要我常到她家打球和游泳，因为她父母亲都忙，游泳池和网球场平常都很少用。我觉得那么好的网球场和游泳池应该好好儿利用，我以后一定要常去她家玩儿。

1. Who is 黄美英? Describe her family and her house.

2. What was the occasion and what did people eat?

3. What are the meanings of 美慕 and 冷清?

4. Do you think 王红 will visit 美英 again and why?

2-3-I Write the characters that contain the given radical for each meaning.

1. 土　earth, soil _____; floor, ground _____; site, address _____; to sit _____

2. 忄　feelings, affection _____; happy, fast, soon _____; busy _____;

to get used to _____

3. 亻　letter (mail) _____; but _____; holiday _____; plural word (people) _____

4. 牛　special _____; object, thing _____; ox, cow _____

5. 宀　guest _____; room _____; character, word _____; free time _____

match, contest _____; home _____; to wear _____; to spoil _____

2-3-J Use the given character to write the words for each meaning.

1. 心　attentive, diligent _____; be careful, take care _____; worry_____;

feel happy, rejoice _____; care about _____;

enthusiastic _____; stop worrying, be at ease _____

2. 分　very, fully, extremely _____; ten minutes _____

3. 半　mostly _____; half _____; half an hour _____

4. 假　spring holiday _____; summer vacation _____;

have a holiday _____; to ask for leave _____

5. 发　ask or raise a question _____; set out, start off _____;

send emails _____; send fax _____; hair _____

第三课　挣零花钱

3-1-A How do you say the following in Chinese? Write in characters wherever possible.

1. Everyone is looking for a job to earn pocket money.

   大家找工作挣零花钱。

2. I found a job at a fast food restaurant last week.

   我上期星在快餐店找到了工作。

3. There are good opportunities for part-time work nowadays.

   最近有很多打工的好机会。

4. She works two hours a day, three days a week.

   她每期星三天，每天两个小时。
   上班

5. After school, he rides a bicycle to a fast food restaurant to work.

   下课后，他骑自行车到快餐店打工。

6. His older sister is coming to pick him up at five o'clock.

   他姐姐在五点来接他。

7. I am so tired that I don't feel like doing anything.

   我很累，所以我不要做什么。

8. Although this job is tiring, the reward is pretty good.

   虽然这个工作累活，回报很好。

9. I felt so good at that moment.

   当我感觉很好。

3-1-B Write the following questions in Chinese and use them to conduct a survey.

Do you have a part-time job? _____

If yes, 1. Why do you have a part-time job? _____

2. What do you do? _____

If no, 1. Why don't you have a job? _____

2. What kind of job would you like to have should there be a chance?

_____

Name	✓ or ✗	why	type of work
(Yourself)			

Answer the following questions according to the results of your survey.

1. 打工的有几个人？

_____

2. 大家最喜欢什么工作？

_____

3-1-C Rearrange the following into proper sentences.

1. 去看电影每次都要同学和钱花。

每次和同学去看电影要花钱。

2. 打工他想是因为零花挣钱。

他想打工因为挣花钱。

3. 不作他工，是老跟要钱父母亲。

他不作工，老是跟父母要钱。

4. 不为什么我知道，作业老是带忘了。

我不知道为什么，老是忘带作业了。

5. 打的工很多机会，好只是的不多工作。

打工的机会很多，只不是好的工作。

6. 学校快餐店对面的正在现在服务员招。

wù　zhāo

快餐店在学校的对面现在招服务员。

7. 一整天我忙了昨天，累得半死。

zhěng　sǐ

我昨天忙了一天整，累得半死。

8. 打是很累工，报回不过不错还。

打工是很累，还不过报回不错。

9. 昨天想她买一衣服件，没刚好带钱可是。

她昨天想买一件衣服，可是没刚好钱。

10. 弟弟得考试第一今天，他妈妈给了拥吻一个。

yōng　wěn

弟弟今天得第一考试他妈妈给一个拥吻。

3-1-D Rewrite the following sentences in Chinese, using 老是 .

1. She always talks in class.

她老是说话。
　在课上

2. He always forgets to bring his book.

他老是忘带他的书。

3. My little brother always logs on to the net to play games.

我弟弟老是上网玩儿电子游戏。

4. He is always naughty in class.

他老是是
　在上课

MAY 1 4 2015

3-1-E Use each word to write a sentence, using as many characters as possible.

1. 流行　这件衣服　流行。

2. 零花钱　我有很多零花钱。

3. 如果　如果你不去，我也不去。

4. 机会　我有很好的机会。

5. 回报　这个是非常好的回报。

6. 刚好　我带了刚好钱。

3-1-F Answer the following questions using complete sentences.

1. 你的零花钱是哪里来的？

是从打工的。

2. 你都怎么用你的零花钱？

？？

3. 你觉得打工的机会多吗？为什么？

打工的机会不多因为^很多店不是找。

4. 他在哪里打工？

在武术学校。

5. 你家附近什么工作机会最多？

我家附近有很多机会

6. 你喜欢打什么工？

我喜欢练习武术。

7. 他的工作时间是什么时候？

是五点五十三分中。

PM

8. 你觉得最好的打工时间是什么时候？

我觉得最好的打工时间是三点。

9. 你觉得这份工作的回报怎么样？

我觉得这份工作的回报很好。

$50/hr

10. 你觉得打工的回报怎么样？

我觉得打工的回报是每小时二十钱。

MAY 1 4 2015

3-1-G There are five jobs and five applicants. Choose an appropriate job for each person and explain the reasons for your choice.

kā fēi wù
咖啡馆服务员，数学老师，书店店员，家教，送报员

姓名	学习、个性	工作	原因
谢大明	学习很认真， 数学很好， 爱踢足球， 喜欢小孩， 很会说话， 很热心		
王美	讨厌数学， 喜欢运动和玩游戏， 喜欢小孩， 钢琴弹得很好， 很外向		
陈明东	功课很好， 喜欢西方菜， 不喜欢小孩， 外向，有人缘儿， 会说汉语		
白小丽	功课不错， 汉语说得很好， 喜欢看书， 外向，热心， 有人缘儿		
马克	学习认真， 数学很好， 喜欢喝咖啡， 内向，不爱说话		

3-1-H　A. You are looking for a job. Read the advertisement and answer the following questions.

周末打工

水果店招店员

工作认真，会说普通话、
热心、外向、人缘儿好

时间：星期六上午九时～下午四时
工资：每小时十八元
电话：1 2 3 4 5 6 7 7
传真：1 2 3 4 5 6 8 8
email: pcworld@msn.com

1. What type of job is this and what is the salary?

2. Are you qualified for this job? Why or why not?

3. Do the hours suit you? Give reasons.

B. Assume the above job does not suit you. Write an advertisement selling yourself. You may include your personality, skills, preferred working hours and ways to contact you.

3-1-I Write the characters that contain the given radical for each meaning.

1. 丨   result, fruit _____; center, middle _____; electricity _____

2. 雨   small amount, zero _____; rain _____; snow _____

3. 足   towards, with, and _____; foot _____; road _____

4. 艹   flower, to spend _____; English _____; medicine _____; festival _____;

        blue _____; tea _____; vegetable, dish _____

5. 纟   paper _____; to practise _____; fate _____; green _____; red _____;

        to pass through _____; grade, level _____; to give _____

6. 氵   to flow _____; alive, to live _____; steam, vapor _____; thirsty _____;

        bay _____; sea _____; Chinese (name of a dynasty) _____; port _____

7. 广   shop _____; should _____; degree _____

3-1-J Use the given character to write the words for each meaning.

1. 果   if _____; fruit _____

2. 回   return, reward _____; letter in reply _____; to go home _____

3. 然   although _____; afterwards, then _____

4. 花   garden _____; pocket money _____

5. 行   in fashion _____; to travel _____; luggage _____

6. 感   feeling _____; moving, touching _____ ; cold, flu _____

3-1-K Listen to the conversation between 王红 and 李大中, then answer the questions.

1. What's the coming event and when is it being held?

2. Where is it taking place and why is it there?

3. What is the working condition mentioned here?

4. Is 大中 able to attend? Give reasons.

Paste here the text given by your teacher and check your understanding. You may also do a role-play with your partner.

3-2-A How do you say the following in Chinese? Write in characters wherever possible.

1. What is the working environment like there?

_____

2. I work as a waiter in a coffee shop.

_____

3. We cannot smoke in our office.

_____

4. I hate being a passive smoker.

_____

5. You are really lucky!

_____

6. My boss has such a bad temper that I can't stand it.

_____

7. My God! That's really unbearable!

_____

8. He always loses his temper.

_____

9. I quit that job last week.

_____

10. This sweater is so cheap that it would be a pity not to buy it.

_____

3-2-B Answer the following questions using complete sentences.

1. 这儿的工作环境怎么样？

_____

2. 这个老板人怎么样？
     ^{bǎn}

_____

3. 这个客人的态度怎么样？
        ^{tài dù}

_____

4. 你看他喜欢他的工作吗？为什么？

_____

5. 你对二手烟的感觉怎么样？
          ^{yān}

_____

6. 他妈妈为什么发脾气？

_____

7. 你爸爸的脾气怎么样？

_____

8. 你觉得你的运气好不好？为什么？

_____

9. 她为什么把工作辞了？
           ^{cí}

_____

10. 什么事最让你受不了？

3-2-C Choose an appropriate word for each sentence, then use that word to write a sentence of your own.

| 到处
chù | 招
zhāo | 二手烟 | 发 | 过 | 虽然 |

1. 学校对面那家书店正在 _____ 店员。

_____

2. 那个公园很脏，_____ 都是垃圾。
   zāng   lā jī

_____

3. 他爸爸很凶，一天到晚 _____ 脾气。
         xiōng

_____

4. 我们班同学多半都打 _____ 工。

_____

5. 他虽然自己不吸烟，但是上班时常常要吸 _____ 。
                          xī yān

_____

3-2-D Rewrite the following sentences in Chinese using 不但……而且…….

1. That book shop not only has a good working environment but also pays a good salary.

_____

2. We not only have too much homework but also have too many exams.

_____

3. He is not only a good teacher but he is also a good father.

_____

3-2-E Find and circle words and phrases.

如 零 跟 刚 态 挺 打 放 份
水 果 花 挣 舒 衣 球 工 顾
曾 书 已 钱 服 累 吸 作 可
最 经 店 务 受 不 了 惜 以
意 服 员 吸 流 行 生 普 板
二 手 烟 电 脾 气 通 而 当
习 环 境 参 说 话 也 关 且

words/phrases	meaning in English		words/phrases	meaning in English
1. _____	_____		2. _____	_____
3. _____	_____		4. _____	_____
5. _____	_____		6. _____	_____
7. _____	_____		8. _____	_____
9. _____	_____		10. _____	_____
11. _____	_____		12. _____	_____
13. _____	_____		14. _____	_____
15. _____	_____		16. _____	_____
17. _____	_____		18. _____	_____
19. _____	_____		20. _____	_____
21. _____	_____		22. _____	_____
23. _____	_____		24. _____	_____
25. _____	_____		26. _____	_____

3-2-F We sometimes come across things which are unbearable. Work with a partner and list them below.

3-2-G Based on the cartoon "退钱" on page 70 in the Textbook, rewrite the story in your own words and provide your comments.

3-2-H Rearrange the following into proper sentences.

1. 最近上班有我们在很多人打工。

_____

2. 最近听说工作找到了你一份。

_____

3. 顾客吸烟多半这咖啡馆的家，到处烟味都是里面。

_____

4. 快餐老板那家店的很客气人，很也员工顾照。

_____

5. 书店这家很好态度都客人的。

_____

6. 餐馆吸烟不让这家，我们所以吸烟不用二手。

_____

7. 我在寒假曾经工作快餐店一家去年。

_____

8. 顾客把那个老是藏东西不付钱起来。

_____

9. 你把不可以用东西坏了再退钱拿回去。

_____

10. 我太忙了学习最近，把很想辞了工作。

_____

3-2-I Write the characters that contain the given radical for each meaning.

1. 心　attitude _____; how _____; to think _____;

to feel, sense _____; you _____

2. 火　cigarette _____; to toast, to grill _____; fever _____; to stir-fry _____

3. ⺍　once, formerly, ever _____; to concern, to close _____; front, before _____;

younger brother _____

4. 月　temper _____; brain _____; fat, plump _____; abdomen _____; clothes

_____; friend _____; a period of time _____; to have, there is/are _____

5. 爫　to love, love _____; to bear, to receive _____

3-2-J Use the given character to write the words for each meaning.

1. 工　have a part-time job _____; to work _____; worker _____

2. 餐　restaurant _____; lunch _____; dinner _____

3. 顾(gù)　look after, take care of _____; customer, client _____

4. 可　it's a pity, too bad _____; can, may _____; lovely _____;

but, however _____

5. 气　temper _____; climate _____; be angry _____; weather _____

6. 度(dù)　attitude _____; go on vacation _____; 15 degrees _____

3-2-K Listen to the conversation between 王红 and 黄美英 , then answer the following questions.

1. Why did 王红 get a part-time job?

2. What is her job and what does she think of it?

3. What advice did 美英 give 王红 and why did she offer the advice?

4. What job is available now and do you think 美英 will get it? Justify your answer.

Paste here the text given by your teacher and check your understanding. You may also do a role-play with your partner.

3-3-A How do you say the following in Chinese? Write in characters wherever possible.

1. I have already saved $200 since I started my part-time work.

_____

2. She saved the $95 her mother gave her.

_____

3. Everything is fine here. You don't need to worry.

_____

4. My mum often nags that I turn up the music too loud.

_____

5. That pair of brand named shoes are very expensive.

_____

6. You really look cool in that pair of trousers.

_____

7. She tried on a skirt and thought it was pretty good.

_____

8. This style is the most popular one this year.

_____

9. The garment is of the best material.

_____

10. He hesitated for a long time, not knowing what to choose.

_____

3-3-B Answer the following questions in complete sentences.

1. 他打工挣来的钱，都用来做什么？

2. 他想存(cún)钱做什么？

3. 他存(cún)了多少钱？他想用来做什么？

4. 你喜欢随身(suí shēn)听吗？你有什么随身(suí shēn)听？

5. 你喜欢把音乐开得很大声(shēng)吗？为什么？

6. 她买衣服都怎么选择(xuǎn zé)？

7. 他妈妈为什么唠叨？

8. 你逛街(guàng jiē)时，什么东西最让你动心？

9. 你买衣服选择料(xuǎn zé liào)子好的还是式(shì)样流行的？为什么？

10. 你父母常唠叨吗？都唠叨些什么？

3-3-C There are many factors which affect our decisions when buying clothes. What are they? Work with a partner to list as many factors as possible.

买还是不买？

买	不买

3-3-D Role-play: One of you is a pushy salesperson at a fashion shop; the other is a fussy customer. Write and practise your script with a partner and then perform the role-play.

_____

_____

_____

_____

_____

3-3-E Write the meaning of each word, then use the word to make a sentence.

meaning   *sentence in Chinese*

1. 唠叨 _____   _____

2. 流行 _____   _____

3. 担心 (dān) _____   _____

4. 逛街 (guàng jiē) _____   _____

5. 名牌 _____   _____

6. 价钱 (jià) _____   _____

7. 动心 _____   _____

8. 犹豫 (yóu yù) _____   _____

9. 实在 (shí) _____   _____

10. 怂恿 (sǒng yǒng) _____   _____

11. 而且 _____   _____

12. 只好 _____   _____

13. 可惜 (xī) _____   _____

14. 曾经 _____   _____

15. 一直 _____   _____

3-3-F Read the story of 王红 who went shopping with 黄美英 , then answer the questions.

美英有一条裤子破了，今天下课后我就陪她去逛街。今天有一家唱片行的唱片很便宜，买一送一。我是摇滚乐迷，一看到唱片，就想买。选了半天，我最后选了四张。买这四张唱片，只付了两张的钱，我觉得实在很便宜。

买了唱片，我们就去逛服饰店。我们逛了四家服饰店，美英试穿了十几条裤子，可是有的太肥，有的太瘦，有的料子不好，有的式样不好看。我拿了一件上衣试穿，还挺合身，挺好看的。虽然料子不怎么好，但是式样很时髦。我很动心，可是又没钱买。美英就一直怂恿我买，她说她可以把钱借给我。犹豫了半天，我还是决定买了。向美英借的钱就等下星期打工挣了钱再还她了，美英的裤子也只好等下次再陪她去买了。

1. Why did they go shopping?

2. What is "买一送一"？

3. What purchases were made today? Describe each decision making process.

4. How do you think 黄美英 felt about this trip? Give reasons for your answer.

3-3-G Complete the following sentences in your own words.

1. 名牌衣服虽然比较贵，_____。

2. 我把打工挣来的零花钱_____。

3. 如果那家书店要招店员_____。
（zhāo）

4. 我犹豫了半天，_____。
（yóu yù）

5. 虽然我喜欢那份工作_____。

6. 如果我存了钱_____。
（cún）

7. 那条裤子不但料子好，_____。
（kù）（liào）

8. 我的老板一天到晚发脾气_____。
（bǎn）

9. 这份工作虽然工资不高_____。
（zī）

10. 我试穿了一件上衣_____。

11. 打工虽然很累_____。

12. 那双鞋不但贵_____。
（shuāng xié）

3-3-H If you won $10,000, how would you spend it ? List five to ten options, specify the amount you would spend on each option and give the reasons for your choices.

For example:

$1,000	给红十字会	帮^{zhù}助别人
$3,000	去中国旅行	去玩儿，也去学习汉语。

多少钱	做什么	为什么
_____	_____	_____
_____	_____	_____
_____	_____	_____
_____	_____	_____
_____	_____	_____
_____	_____	_____
_____	_____	_____
_____	_____	_____
_____	_____	_____

3-3-I Write the characters that contain the given radical for each meaning.

1. 口　　to inhale _____; to nag _____or_____; question words _____or_____;

towards, to _____; although _____; to drink _____; may, approve _____;

where, which _____; to vomit, to spit _____

2. 方　　room _____; to put, to let go _____; square, direction_____; to travel _____

3. 人　　can _____; measure word _____; present (time) _____; from _____

4. 夕　　famous, name _____; outside _____; many, much _____

5. 钅　　money _____; wrong, incorrect _____; time, clock _____

6. 刂　　don't, distinction, other _____; just now, just _____; play, drama _____

7. 女　　mother _____; to start, to begin _____; family name _____; if _____;

mother's sister _____; good _____; younger sister _____;

older sister _____

8. 广　　shop _____; should _____; degree _____

9. 扌　　to shoulder, to bear _____; newspaper, to report _____; to earn _____;

to pick up _____; grammatical word _____; to exchange _____;

quite, very _____

第四课　年轻人的世界

4-1-A How do you say the following in Chinese? Write in characters wherever possible.

1. You gave me a fright!

_____

2. I am very tired today and unable to read any books.

_____

3. My older sister broke up with her boyfriend yesterday.

_____

4. I feel that our personalities are incompatible.

_____

5. He is tall, handsome and a prince charming in the eyes of every girl.

_____

6. His uncle is very arrogant and pays no respect to others.

_____

7. After a fight last night, both of us decided to say goodbye.

_____

8. We broke up, but it is no big deal.

_____

9. Her mother does not approve of her having a boyfriend now.

_____

4-1-B Write your questions and conduct a survey to find out what kind of girlfriend/ boyfriend your classmates would like to have. Write your ideal type on the first line.

Q1. _____

Q2. _____

Name	**Physical appearance**	**Personality**
(Yourself)		

Answer the following questions according to the results of your survey.

1. 大家最喜欢的是长得怎么样的人？

男: _____

女: _____

2. 大家最不喜欢什么样的个性？

_____

4-1-C Answer the following questions in complete sentences.

1. 你看她在做什么？

_____

2. 你常发呆_{dāi}吗？为什么？

_____

3. 你心情不好的时候都做什么？

_____

4. 你心目^{mù}中的男／女朋友是什么样的人？

_____

5. 在你家人中，谁和你个性最不合^{hé}？

_____

6. 你跟人吵^{chǎo}过架^{jià}吗？为了什么吵架？

_____

7. 你们班上谁最出风头？他／她为什么出风头？

_____

8. 你曾经大哭过吗？是为了什么事？

_____

9. 你的父母亲赞不赞成你现在交男／女朋友？为什么？

_____

10. 你将^{jiāng}来想上大学吗？为什么？

_____

4-1-D Choose an appropriate word for each sentence, then use that word to write a sentence.

| 赞成　才　把　出风头　心目中　发呆　大不了　就　吹 |

1. 钱丢了 ＿＿＿＿＿ 丢了，别难过了。

＿＿＿＿＿＿＿＿＿＿＿＿＿＿＿＿＿＿＿＿＿＿＿＿

2. 跟女朋友吵架是小事，没什么 ＿＿＿＿＿ 的。

＿＿＿＿＿＿＿＿＿＿＿＿＿＿＿＿＿＿＿＿＿＿＿＿

3. 他很爱 ＿＿＿＿＿ ，班上同学都不喜欢他。

＿＿＿＿＿＿＿＿＿＿＿＿＿＿＿＿＿＿＿＿＿＿＿＿

4. 他学习好，又很热心，是老师 ＿＿＿＿＿ 的好学生。

＿＿＿＿＿＿＿＿＿＿＿＿＿＿＿＿＿＿＿＿＿＿＿＿

5. 姐姐昨天和男朋友 ＿＿＿＿＿ 了？

＿＿＿＿＿＿＿＿＿＿＿＿＿＿＿＿＿＿＿＿＿＿＿＿

6. 妈妈不 ＿＿＿＿＿ 我现在交男朋友。

＿＿＿＿＿＿＿＿＿＿＿＿＿＿＿＿＿＿＿＿＿＿＿＿

7. 他太骄傲了，都不 ＿＿＿＿＿ 别人放在眼里。

＿＿＿＿＿＿＿＿＿＿＿＿＿＿＿＿＿＿＿＿＿＿＿＿

8. 你得好好儿准备，考试 ＿＿＿＿＿ 能考得好。

＿＿＿＿＿＿＿＿＿＿＿＿＿＿＿＿＿＿＿＿＿＿＿＿

9. 他上课不用心，常常坐着 ＿＿＿＿＿ 。

＿＿＿＿＿＿＿＿＿＿＿＿＿＿＿＿＿＿＿＿＿＿＿＿

4-1-E Read each of the following opinions and decide whether the person agrees with the idea of having a boyfriend/girlfriend. Give the reasons for your answer.

他们赞成中学生交男／女朋友吗？

✓ or ✗　　　Why?

Maria

我和以前的男朋友常吵架（chǎo jià）。每次一吵架，我心里就很难过，学习也不用心。上次和男朋友分手以后，我又难过得不得了，考试考得很差。现在我决定上大学以前不再交男朋友了。

Charlie

我认为交女朋友很好，可以学习到很多女孩子和男孩子的不同。

Anna

我和我的男朋友常常在一起做功课。我们很谈得来，每次聊天都聊得很开心。我觉得晚上出去的时候，有男朋友保护，也挺（tǐng）不错的。

David

有了女朋友就要请她看电影或陪（péi）她出去玩儿，很浪费（làng fèi）时间。我希望多利用时间好好儿学习，所以我不交女朋友。

Peter

我的女朋友功课很好。我们常常一块儿学习。现在我的功课比以前好多了。

Julie

我父母认为中学生应该好好儿学习，不应该交男朋友。我觉得他们说得很对，其实我打算一辈（bèi）子不结婚（jié hūn）。

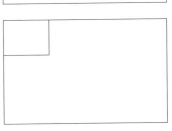

4-1-F There are times when we get bored. List the thoughts that may occur to you when you are bored.

4-1-G Rewrite the following sentences in Chinese, using 才.

1. My young brother is only six years old.

_____

2. It is still early; it is only five o'clock.

_____

3. Walk faster so that we won't be late.

_____

4. You must do your homework so that the teacher will not get angry.

_____

5. I started waiting for him at 3:00pm but he did not arrive until 4:30pm.

_____

4-1-H Rearrange the following into proper sentences.

1. 我不好今天情心，什么下去看不书都。

　　_____

2. 去功课快做，那儿坐在别呆了发。（dāi）

　　_____

3. 你了玩笑开别！

　　_____

4. 他女孩子是每个白马心目中的王子。（mù　wáng）

　　_____

5. 他好得网球打，上球场在风头出很。

　　_____

6. 骄她很傲，都不眼里别把人放在。（jiāo　ào　yǎn）

　　_____

7. 爸爸架和吵了以后昨天，我很一直难过觉得。（jià　chǎo）

　　_____

8. 分手女朋友分手了就和，大没不了什么的。（liǎo）

　　_____

9. 赞成我不现在妈妈女朋友交。

　　_____

10. 老师我们要学习好好儿，将来大学考上才能好的。（jiǎng）

　　_____

4-1-I Write the characters that contain the given radical for each meaning.

1. 冫　to decide _____; standard, accurate _____; cool _____; cold _____

2. 木　shelf, rack _____; board _____; technique, art _____; photograph _____;

aircraft, machine _____; multistorey building _____; appearance _____

3. 八　that, such _____; pleasure _____; together _____;

to divide, minute, cent _____

4. 又　diffcult _____; correct _____; happy _____; uncle _____;

friend _____; pair _____; hair _____

5. 贝　to support _____; expensive _____

6. 口　noisy, to quarrel _____; to blow _____; to inhale _____; to sing _____

4-1-J Use the given character to write the words for each meaning.

1. 通　Mandarin _____; usually _____; transportation _____

2. 过　sad _____; to go past _____; to come over _____

3. 认　think that... _____; conscientious _____

4. 成　agree with _____; become _____; adult _____

5. 出　be in the spotlight _____; exit _____; to go out _____

6. 个　personality _____; height _____; two people _____

7. 手　break up _____; to be good at _____; wristwatch _____

4-2-A How do you say the following in Chinese? Write in characters wherever possible.

1. Lately my little brother often lies.

_____

2. Did you smoke? Answer honestly.

_____

3. My parents do not allow me to smoke.

_____

4. Don't worry. No one saw me coming.

_____

5. Exercise is good for your health.

_____

6. Taking drugs is harmful to your health.

_____

7. It is easy to start smoking but difficult to quit.

_____

8. At the beginning he only smoked for fun but then he became addicted to it.

_____

9. Whether or not you go to university is up to you.

_____

10. Don't make a mountain out of a molehill.

_____

4-2-B Answer the following questions using complete sentences.

1. 你说过谎^{huǎng}吗？当时的感觉怎么样？

_____

2. 他为什么抽烟^{chōu yān}？

_____

3. 他为什么吸毒^{xī dú}？

_____

4. 抽烟^{chōu yān}对身体怎么样？

_____

5. 你认为年轻人为什么吸毒^{xī dú}？

_____

6. 如果有人怂恿^{sǒng yǒng}你吸毒，你怎么办^{bàn}？

_____

7. 如果看到朋友抽烟^{chōu yān}，你怎么办？

_____

8. 她对什么上了瘾^{yǐn}？

_____

9. 你对什么上了瘾？

_____

10. 你最大的毛病是什么？

_____

4-2-C Choose an appropriate word for each sentence, then use that word to write a sentence.

而已	到	一旦 dàn	麻烦 má fán

1. 我在爸爸的书房找 ＿＿＿＿＿＿ 了我的随身听。
suí

＿＿＿＿＿＿＿＿＿＿＿＿＿＿＿＿＿＿＿＿＿＿＿＿＿＿＿＿＿＿＿＿

2. 没问题，这是小事，一点都不 ＿＿＿＿＿＿ 。
wèn

＿＿＿＿＿＿＿＿＿＿＿＿＿＿＿＿＿＿＿＿＿＿＿＿＿＿＿＿＿＿＿＿

3. 一个人 ＿＿＿＿＿＿ 上了毒瘾，就戒不掉了。
dú yǐn　　jiè diào

＿＿＿＿＿＿＿＿＿＿＿＿＿＿＿＿＿＿＿＿＿＿＿＿＿＿＿＿＿＿＿＿

4. 我不买，只是看看 ＿＿＿＿＿＿ 。

＿＿＿＿＿＿＿＿＿＿＿＿＿＿＿＿＿＿＿＿＿＿＿＿＿＿＿＿＿＿＿＿

4-2-D Use the following words/phrases to make sentences.

1. 明明 ＿＿＿＿＿＿＿＿＿＿＿＿＿＿＿＿＿＿＿＿＿＿＿＿＿＿＿＿＿＿

2. 老实说来 ＿＿＿＿＿＿＿＿＿＿＿＿＿＿＿＿＿＿＿＿＿＿＿＿＿＿＿

3. 麻烦 ＿＿＿＿＿＿＿＿＿＿＿＿＿＿＿＿＿＿＿＿＿＿＿＿＿＿＿＿＿
má fán

4. 容易 ＿＿＿＿＿＿＿＿＿＿＿＿＿＿＿＿＿＿＿＿＿＿＿＿＿＿＿＿＿

5. 上瘾 ＿＿＿＿＿＿＿＿＿＿＿＿＿＿＿＿＿＿＿＿＿＿＿＿＿＿＿＿＿
yǐn

6. 小心 ＿＿＿＿＿＿＿＿＿＿＿＿＿＿＿＿＿＿＿＿＿＿＿＿＿＿＿＿＿

7. 小题大做 ＿＿＿＿＿＿＿＿＿＿＿＿＿＿＿＿＿＿＿＿＿＿＿＿＿＿

4-2-E Rearrange the following into proper sentences.

1. 心你放，我到没人烟看抽。

_____

2. 身体抽烟有对害，瘾一旦上麻烦了就。

_____

3. 吸和抽烟都上瘾毒很容易。

_____

4. 烟容吸易，烟难戒。

_____

5. 一旦上了瘾一个人毒，不就戒掉了。

_____

6. 气你生别，我开只是已而玩笑。

_____

7. 我只是好玩抽烟抽着而已，瘾不会上的。

_____

8. 烟不抽抽，一切你自己在于。

_____

9. 她爱人这个最了大小做题。

_____

10. 你有了是不是男朋友？老说实来快！

4-2-F Find and circle words, phrases and expressions.

中 学 习 很 认 真 的 吗
吵 照 顾 生 忙 受 吃 吹
架 别 客 气 得 不 得 了
没 什 么 大 不 了 很 害
问 难 过 平 关 放 过 上
题 刮 非 常 开 心 瘾 一
出 风 头 发 交 换 学 生

words/phrases	meaning in English	words/phrases	meaning in English
1. _____ _____		2. _____ _____	
3. _____ _____		4. _____ _____	
5. _____ _____		6. _____ _____	
7. _____ _____		8. _____ _____	
9. _____ _____		10. _____ _____	
11. _____ _____		12. _____ _____	
13. _____ _____		14. _____ _____	
15. _____ _____		16. _____ _____	
17. _____ _____		18. _____ _____	
19. _____ _____		20. _____ _____	
21. _____ _____		22. _____ _____	
23. _____ _____		24. _____ _____	

4-2-G Complete the following sentences in your own words.

1. 你今天明明没吃早饭 _____。

2. 他昨天明明抽烟了，^{chōu yān} _____。

3. 我只是买了一件衣服而已，_____。

4. 那个苹果我才吃了一口，^{píng} _____。

5. 他昨天十二点半才睡觉，^{shuì} _____。

6. 这本书我看不下去，_____。

7. 他很爱出风头，_____。

8. 书丢就丢了，^{diū} _____。

9. 一个人抽烟一旦上了瘾 ^{chōu yān} ^{dàn} ^{yǐn} _____。

10. 他只是开玩笑而已 _____。

11. 我抽烟只是抽着好玩而已 ^{chōu yān} _____。

12. 我觉得最容易上瘾的是 ^{yǐn} _____。

4-2-H Write the characters that contain the given radical for each meaning.

1. 戈　　quit, give up _____; to become, to succeed _____; I, me _____

2. 疒　　addiction, strong interest _____; sick, illness _____; thin _____; ache _____

3. 亻　　body _____; letter (mail) _____; but _____; m.w. for job, report _____

4. 宀　　harm _____; to hold, appearance _____; finish _____; truth _____;

　　　　to decide, certain _____;　home _____; to wear _____

5. 日　　easy _____; general, common _____; star _____; the most _____;

　　　　early, morning _____; heat, hot weather _____; spring _____; warm _____

6. 页　　topic, question _____; to attend to _____

7. 母　　poison, toxin _____; every, each _____; mother _____

4-2-I Use the given character to write the words for each meaning.

1. 烟　to smoke _____; cigarette _____; passive smoking _____;
   ^{yān}

　　　quit smoking _____

2. 准　not allow, forbid _____; prepare _____; punctual, on time _____

3. 实　honest _____; actually _____; really _____

4. 上　be addicted to _____; get on the internet _____;

　　　the largest city in China _____; upper garment _____

4-2-J Listen to the conversation between 李大中 and 王红, then answer the following questions.

1. What did 王红 discover?

2. How did 李大中 react to 王红's discovery?

3. What worried 王红 regarding this discovery?

4. How did 李大中 justify it and how was it concluded?

Paste here the copy of the conversation given by your teacher and check your understanding.

4-2-K Your Chinese friend takes up smoking and his mother is very upset. Write him an email to convince him to quit.

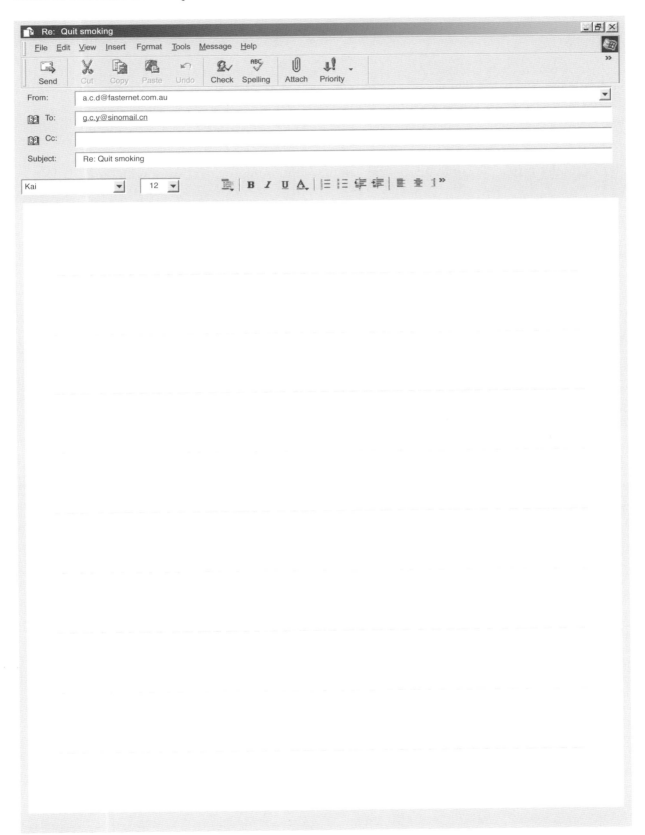

4-3-A　How do you say the following in Chinese? Write in characters wherever possible.

1. Someone suggested that we dye our hair, but no one agreed.

_____

2. Someone suggested that we go to a movie, and we all agreed.

_____

3. Originally I didn't want to go, but my friends kept urging me so I went with them.

_____

4. After having my hair dyed red, I felt weird.

_____

5. Every day mum starts nagging as soon as I come home.

_____

6. My younger brother told dad about my tattoos.

_____

7. I feel that I am pretty conservative and not at all fashionable.

_____

8. My mum is not open-minded at all. She will not let me go to dances.

_____

9. To be honest, it's pretty inconvenient wearing belly button rings.

_____

10. I am in a dilemma and don't know what to do.

_____

4-3-B Rewrite the following sentences in Chinese, using the format "v + 成".

1. She dyed her hair purple.

_____

2. She altered her trousers into shorts.

_____

3. He always says '水饺' as '睡觉^{shuì}'.

_____

4-3-C Rearrange the following into proper sentences.

1. 他去要本来，可是有事因为去临^{lín}时不能。

_____

2. 爸爸去中国暑假旅行提议^{tí yì}，妈妈可是赞成不。

_____

3. 弟发染^{rǎn}弟把头成色的红，妈他爱作妈骂^{mà}怪。

_____

4. 都说同学们打扮^{bàn}我今天的很新潮^{cháo}，我觉得但是不。

_____

5. 开我妈妈很虽然通，也会叨唠有时候但是。

_____

6. 不太好天气今天，会下雨可能下午。

_____

4-3-D There are many things we often complain about. Work with your partner and list the complaints you both have.

4-3-E We often complain about our parents' nagging. Work with a partner and list the things that your parents usually nag about.

4-3-F Answer the following questions in complete sentences.

1. 你逛街时最常做什么？

_____

2. 你染^{rǎn}不染头发？为什么？

2. 你染不染头发？为什么？

_____

3. 你想不想戴肚脐环？为什么？

_____

4. 如果你的朋友怂恿你做不该做的事，你怎么办？

_____

5. 你父母曾经跟你大发脾气吗？是为了什么事？

_____

6. 你觉得现在的年轻人很爱作怪吗？为什么？

_____

7. 你曾经小题大做吗？是为了什么事？

_____

8. 你做过奇怪的打扮吗？怎么打扮？

_____

9. 你的家人中谁最保守？你为什么这么认为？

_____

10. 什么事曾经让你心里觉得矛盾？后来怎么样？

4-3-G Describe a person who dresses in the most unusual fashion. Use an illustration to help you. Then answer the following questions.

		(Illustration)
头发		
衣服		
其他		

1. 你自己做不做这样的打^{bàn}扮？为什么？

2. 如果你做这样的打扮，你父母会赞成吗？为什么？

3. 你平常都怎么打扮？

4-3-H Use the following words/phrases to make sentences.

1. máo dùn
矛盾　_____

2. tí yì
提议　_____

3. 赞成　_____

4. sǒng yǒng
怂恿　_____

5. 怪怪的　_____

6. jiū jìng
究竟　_____

7. 作怪　_____

8. 一……就　_____

9. bàn
打扮　_____

10. shǒu
保守　_____

11. 开通　_____

12. cháo
新潮　_____

4-3-I Read the following passage about 王红 and answer the following questions.

　　上个星期天下午，我和姐姐一起去逛街。姐姐临时提议去穿耳洞。我本来不想去，因为我不想花钱，又怕疼，可是姐姐说她要付钱，所以我就跟着去了。穿了耳洞，戴上了耳环，我觉得看起来还挺好看的，只是我的耳朵一直热热的，很不舒服。姐姐要我放心，说过几天就会没事的。后来我们看到一家美容院，姐姐又提议去染头发。我有点儿犹豫，可是姐姐一直怂恿，也就跟着进去了。我们俩都把头发染成金色的，看起来挺酷的。我很开心，可是又有点矛盾，因为妈妈一定会唠叨，说我们爱作怪。不过姐姐说没关系，妈妈唠叨就让她唠叨了。

1. When did the events take place and how did things start?

2. What did 王红's sister suggest to do and what was 王红's reaction?

3. How did 王红 feel after each event?

4. How did 王红's sister react to her feelings?

4-3-J Write the characters that contain the given radical for each meaning.

1. 扌　put on, play the part of _____; smoke, take out _____; to shoulder, to bear

_____; to look for _____; to pull, to play _____; row, to line up _____

2. 忄　odd, strange _____; character, nature _____; to have pity on _____;

feelings, affection _____; to get used to _____; fast, soon _____;

busy _____

3. 一　even, more _____; also, moreover _____; world _____; just _____;

again _____; business, matter _____; to come _____; east _____

4. 厂　oppose _____; shield _____; behind, after _____; toilet _____;

experience, history _____

5. 辶　to stroll _____; to choose, to elect, choice _____;

through, to get through _____; way _____; to transport, luck _____;

side _____; also, still _____; to pass, cross _____

6. 车　light (in weight) _____; vehicle _____; to compare _____

7. 夂　place _____; to prepare _____; every, each _____; winter _____;

slip, measure word for long object _____; summer _____

8. 大　strange _____; head _____; big _____; sky _____; too, exceedingly _____

4-3-K Listen to the conversation between 李大中 and 王红 , then answer the following questions.

1. What happened to 张南 and why did it happen?

2. What was 王红's impression of 张南?

3. What's 大中's opinion of 张南?

4. What worries 王红 about 张南 ?

Paste here the copy of the conversation given by your teacher to check your understanding.

写 字 练 习

How to write a character correctly:

1. Write the strokes according to the numbered sequence.
2. Start each stroke beginning where the number is located.
3. End a stroke with the pen lifted off the paper if it has a pointed end, or with the pen stopped on the paper if it has a round end.

Trace the two lightly printed examples and maintain the proportions in the practice boxes.
The first space is for you to write the Pinyin and meaning of each character.

1

		Pinyin: Meaning:							
	才	才 才							
		P: M:							
	放	放 放							
		P: M:							
	非	非 非							
		P: M:							
	心	心 心							
		P: M:							
	新	新 新							
		P: M:							
	姓	姓 姓							
		P: M:							
	听	听 听							

	P: M:							
教	教 教							
认	P: M:							
	认 认							
关	P: M:							
	关 关							
把	P: M:							
	把 把							
当	P: M:							
	当 当							
忙	P: M:							
	忙 忙							
活	P: M:							
	活 活							
帮	P: M:							
	帮 帮							
谈	P: M:							
	谈 谈							

成	P: M:	成	成						
每	P: M:	每	每						
己	P: M:	己	己						
除	P: M:	除	除						
着	P: M:	着	着						
正	P: M:	正	正						
虽	P: M:	虽	虽						
然	P: M:	然	然						
但	P: M:	但	但						

	P: M:	网	网							
	P: M:	邮	邮							
	P: M:	聊	聊							
	P: M:	室	室							
	P: M:	脑	脑							
	P: M:	功	功							
	P: M:	应	应							
	P: M:	该	该							
	P: M:	利	利							

网邮聊室脑功应该利

		P: M:							
用		用	用						
位		P: M:							
		位	位						
各		P: M:							
		各	各						
印		P: M:							
		印	印						
象		P: M:							
		象	象						
告		P: M:							
		告	告						
诉		P: M:							
		诉	诉						
通		P: M:							
		通	通						
世		P: M:							
		世	世						

界

种

惯

园

烤

肉

父

母

亲

界 界

种 种

惯 惯

园 园

烤 烤

肉 肉

父 父

母 母

亲 亲

P:
M:

	P: M:							
希	希 希							

	P: M:							
望	望 望							

	P: M:							
牛	牛 牛							

	P: M:							
拾	拾 拾							

	P: M:							
它	它 它							

	P: M:							
环	环 环							

	P: M:							
保	保 保							

	P: M:							
切	切 切							

	P: M:							
封	封 封							

游	P: M:							
	游 游							
泳	P: M:							
	泳 泳							
特	P: M:							
	特 特							
护	P: M:							
	护 护							
流	P: M:							
	流 流							
工	P: M:							
	工 工							
挣	P: M:							
	挣 挣							
零	P: M:							
	零 零							
花	P: M:							
	花 花							

或

餐

店

员

报

纸

份

累

刚

P:
M:
或　或

P:
M:
餐　餐

P:
M:
店　店

P:
M:
员　员

P:
M:
报　报

P:
M:
纸　纸

P:
M:
份　份

P:
M:
累　累

P:
M:
刚　刚

受	P: M:	受	受						
境	P: M:	境	境						
让	P: M:	让	让						
曾	P: M:	曾	曾						
而	P: M:	而	而						
且	P: M:	且	且						
脾	P: M:	脾	脾						
从	P: M:	从	从						
唠	P: M:	唠	唠						

	P: M:										
叨	叨	叨									
进	P: M:										
	进	进									
名	P: M:										
	名	名									
牌	P: M:										
	牌	牌									
条	P: M:										
	条	条									
定	P: M:										
	定	定									
直	P: M:										
	直	直									
情	P: M:										
	情	情									
吹	P: M:										
	吹	吹									

4

实	P: M:									
	实 实									
决	P: M:									
	决 决									
笑	P: M:									
	笑 笑									
处	P: M:									
	处 处									
出	P: M:									
	出 出									
孩	P: M:									
	孩 孩									
其	P: M:									
	其 其									
难	P: M:									
	难 难									
哭	P: M:									
	哭 哭									

反	P: M:							
赞	反	反						
赞	P: M:							
借	赞	赞						
借	P: M:							
身	借	借						
身	P: M:							
体	身	身						
体	P: M:							
害	体	体						
害	P: M:							
容	害	害						
容	P: M:							
易	容	容						
易	P: M:							
死	易	易						
死	P: M:							
	死	死						

完

爱

题

包

逛

街

美

怪

轻

P:
M:

P:
M:

P:
M:

P:
M:

P:
M:

P:
M:

P:
M:

P:
M:

P:
M:

奇

奇 奇

P:
M:

P:
M:

P:
M:

P:
M:

P:
M:

P:
M:

P:
M:

P:
M:

	P: M:							
	P: M:							
	P: M:							
	P: M:							
	P: M:							
	P: M:							
	P: M:							
	P: M:							
	P: M:							